4

dedicated to

the noted author and a recognized pioneer of

OrigamiUSA

FLORENCE TEMKO

for whom the art of paperfolding

is a joy to share

ORIGAMI
MASTERWORKS
Innovative Forms in the Art of Paperfolding

Design and Editing   MARTHA W. LONGENECKER

Editing   ROB SIDNER

Photography   LYNTON GARDINER

A MINGEI INTERNATIONAL EXHIBITION DOCUMENTARY

Made possible by an Anonymous Benefactress

frontispieces

ORIGAMI ABSTRACTS

Paul Jackson

Israel

approximate size

page 4

UNITED WE STAND (1000 CRANES)

Mark Morden

U.S.A.

37" h

pages 6, 8-9,10

WHIRLPOOL PATTERN

Tomoko Fusé

Japan

lengths: 31 1/2", 15 1/8", 13 1/2"

page 7

ROSY FINCH

Robert J. Lang

U.S.A.

actual size

ISBN 0914155-18-0

LIBRARY OF CONGRESS CONTROL NUMBER: 2003112170

PUBLISHED BY MINGEI INTERNATIONAL MUSEUM
BALBOA PARK 1439 EL PRADO SAN DIEGO CA 92101
MAILING ADDRESS PO BOX 553 LA JOLLA CA 92038

CONTENTS

FOREWORD

Martha W. Longenecker
Founding President and Director, Mingei International Museum

A piece of origami in our hands is a small form of one of mankind's remarkable achievements – paper. It is hard to conceive of a world without paper – a manmade material often taken for granted as a disposable product. Yet, pausing to consider, we realize how remarkable is this material invented in China by the first century B.C.

Prior to the use of paper for writing, early civilizations used materials such as stone, bone, wood and clay, as well as parchment and papyrus.

Paper made from plant fibers could be recycled and was not only pliable but also foldable and creasable without cracking or tearing, unlike papyrus which needed to be kept flat or rolled.

From China, where papermaking had been kept secret, it slowly spread via trade routes to neighboring Korea, Japan and along the silk road to the Middle East, from where the Moors took it to Spain in the 12th century.

Paper's development into multiple sheets of unified size and thickness was key to the invention of the printing press that began Europe's cultural revolution in the 15th century.

Paper is now made world wide in a seemingly endless variety of weights, thickness, colors, textures and translucency and used for numerous purposes including newspapers, wrappers, textiles, writing papers – and origami!

UNTITLED
Jean-Claude Corriea
France

14 1/2" h

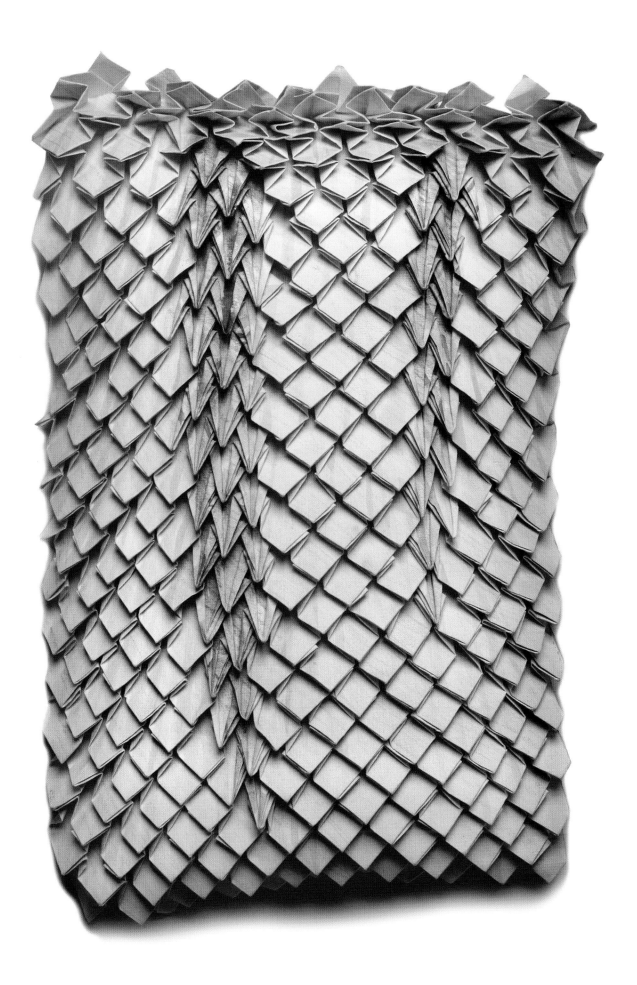

It is not known who was the first person to fold a flat piece of paper into a three-dimensional form. However, I would imagine that it was a creative Chinese person, handling this extraordinary material soon after its invention. What an exhilarating moment that must have been! Even now a paper folder may experience similar joy.

Shortly after its establishment in 1978, Mingei International Museum was blessed with a member who had an infectious enthusiasm for paper — Florence Temko, author of many books on origami. Her donation to our Museum of her International paper collection and library on paper (now housed at the Museum in Balboa Park, San Diego) was the impetus for Mingei International's 1985 traveling exhibition entitled, *PAPER INNOVATIONS* – Handmade Paper and Handmade Objects of Cut, Folded and Molded Paper.

While serving as a Curatoral Consultant for that exhibition, she proposed to help Mingei International organize an entire origami exhibition to be coordinated with a future OrigamiUSA conference in San Diego.

Now, 18 years later, the time has come! *ORIGAMI MASTERWORKS — Innovative Forms in the Art of Paperfolding* is the centerpiece for OrigamiUSA's Pacific Coast Conference, held in San Diego, October 9-13, 2003. Guest Curator for the exhibition is V'Ann Cornelius, Remote Vice President of OrigamiUSA.

This publication is a timeless documentary of the exhibition which is composed of a broad representation of contemporary origami designs developed during the past 50 years. It features the work of internationally recognized origami artists, authors and leaders.

KOI
Robert J. Lang
U.S.A.
11" l

All the members of Mingei International's Board of Trustees join me in thanking:

The Anonymous Benefactress, whose generous grant made possible this publication and the exhibition documentary film

Members of Mingei International's Director's Circle, who provide the core support for the Museum's international exhibition program

Florence Temko, Curatoral Consultant, who planted and nurtured the seed

V'Ann Cornelius, Remote Vice President of OrigamiUSA, for serving as the Exhibition Guest Curator, and working through the years to bring the vision to fruition

Anthony Cheng, President of OrigamiUSA, and other members of the Board of Directors for their coordinated planning

The creators and folders of origami represented in the exhibition. Additional thanks to the origami artists who contributed their pieces to Mingei International's permanent collection so that they might become part of a traveling exhibition for an ever widening audience

The Museum Staff – who actualize the vision, quietly, skillfully, joyfully

The Volunteers and Docents and all who enrich the museum program

KOI
Michael G. La Fosse
U.S.A.

6 1/2" l

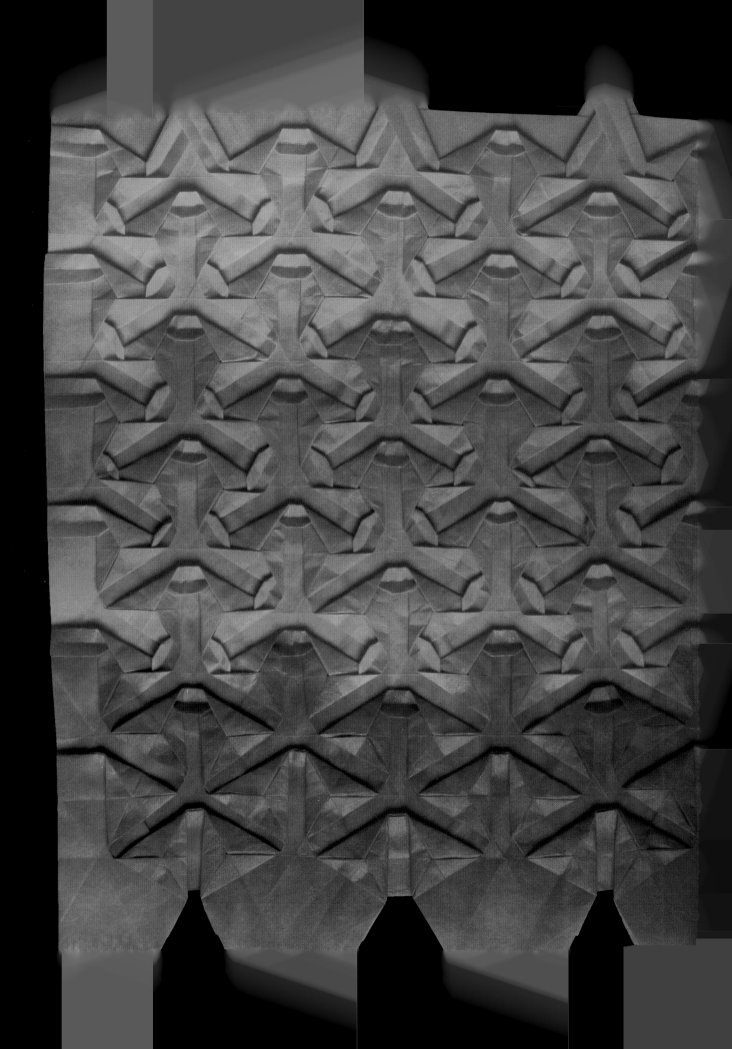

COMMENTARY

V'Ann Cornelius
Exhibition Guest Curator

O rigami is inviting, mysterious, and magical. A flat piece of paper is folded to produce shapes and forms that surprise the eye!

Origami techniques explore the nature of a paper's surface, bringing change without adding to or subtracting from its original form. The processes can be reduced to two movements — bending the paper up or bending the paper down. The unfolded origami reveals a crease pattern of mountain and valley folds.

A paperfolder begins an origami form by selecting a piece of paper for its color, texture, size, and other qualities. The folder holds and handles the paper, considering its weight and strength, as well as its capacity to hold a crease.

Through observing the pattern of creases and experimenting with simple forms, the beginner learns how paper responds to different folding sequences. With time and skill, the folding can take on an aspect similar to the choreography of dance — movement of hands and paper in time and space.

It is a privilege to work with paper in creating sculptural forms akin to songs or poems. What seemingly was not possible becomes real. A flat piece of paper transforms into a tangible form — a dragon, a bird in flight — and possibly even an object of art.

WHIRLPOOL PATTERN
Tomoko Fusé
Japan
10 1/2" h

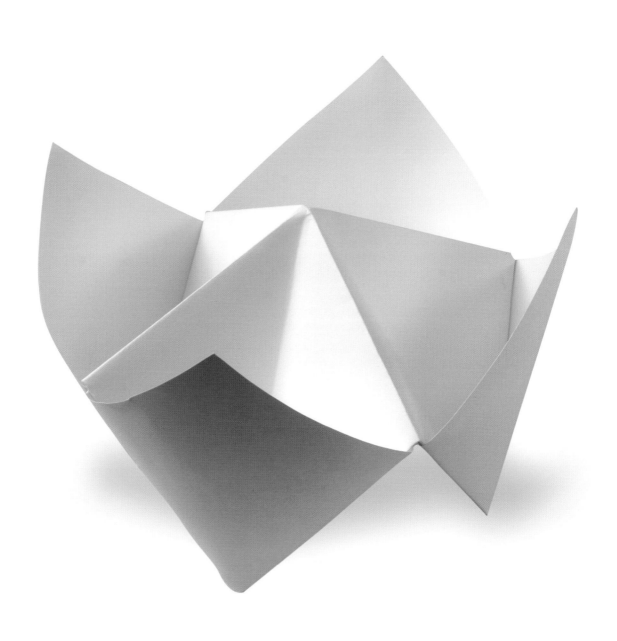

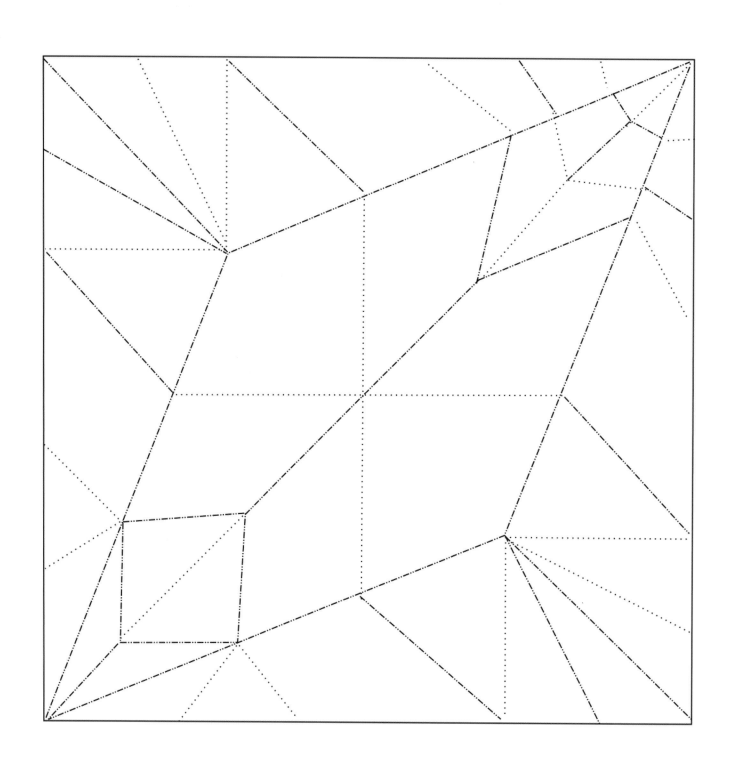

CREASE PATTERN AND FOLDING SEQUENCE FOR ROOSTER

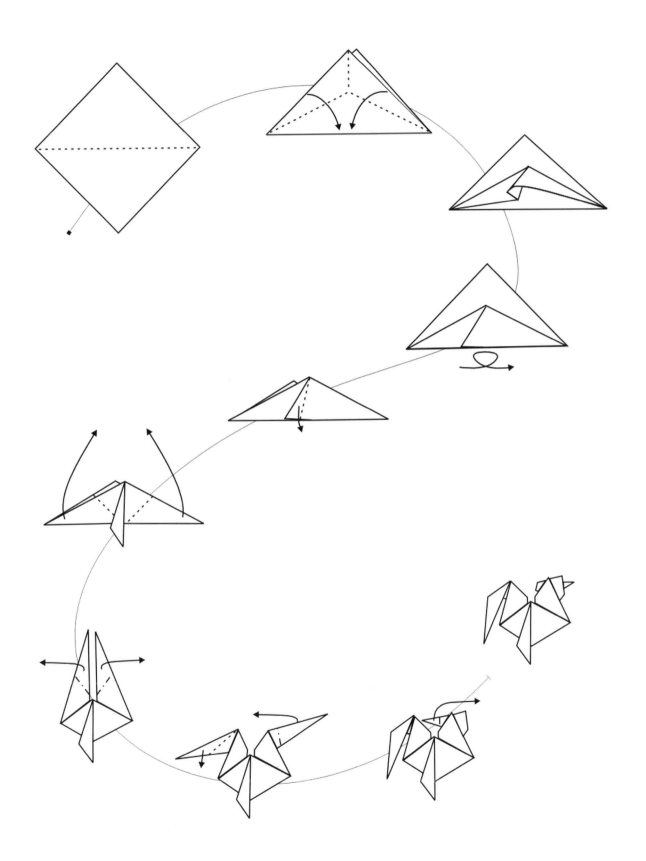

ORIGAMI — A BACKGROUND

Florence Temko

O rigami, the art of folding paper, is now enjoyed by many people in many countries for amusement, as an educational tool and as an art form.

In traditional origami, squares of paper are folded into decorations, animals, objects and sculptures in a limitless variety. Many cultures include one or more such paper objects among their traditions. The paper airplane immediately comes to mind, as well as the hat made from a sheet of newspaper. The Japanese crane has universal appeal, and in Spain the little bird called the *pajarita* is well known.

More so than in any other country, origami is part of the culture of Japan. For this reason origami is often thought to be a Japanese art. The Japanese word "origami" translates as paper folding, *ori* meaning to fold, and *gami* meaning paper. As in most Asian arts, traditional origami includes cultural motifs which relate to deep-seated symbolism. For example, the crane, which lives to a great age, represents good wishes for a long life. Butterflies are associated with Japanese weddings as symbols of happiness in marriage.

It is believed that paper folding may have been used in Japan for ceremonial rites as early as the year 1000, but conclusive evidence is lacking. Folded paper is certainly part of Japanese religious observances to this day. Beginning during the Heian period (794-1191) and the later Muromachi (1333-1573) and Edo periods (1603-1867), origami became a recreational pastime for the wealthy who created many new folded shapes. With the increased availability of paper, origami gift wrapping, letters, boxes, animal forms and other figures became popular.

ROOSTER
Florence Temko
U.S.A.

actual size

27

When Japan's isolation ceased at the beginning of the Meiji Restoration (1868-1912), cultural interchanges between East and West began. Solid evidence of the beginnings of paperfolding in Europe is lacking, but in the 17th century in Central Europe baptismal certificates folded from decorated squares were not unusual. Other indications from England and Italy suggest that isolated forms of paperfolding appeared there at the time.

In the early 19th century, the German educator and founder of the Kindergarten, Friedrich Froebel (1782-1852), included paperfolding in the basic school curriculum to introduce children to mathematical and geometrical concepts.

Although the origins of origami reach well into past centuries, during the last 50 years it has grown as a recreational craft with international impact. A major impetus to origami as it is now practiced began in the late 1950s.

Lillian Oppenheimer in the United States and Robert Harbin in England, among others, stimulated public awareness, which resulted in the formation of paperfolding societies in many countries. The famous Japanese paperfolder, Akira Yoshizawa, now in his 91st year, dominated the transformation of origami into a publicly recognized art form.

Origami is often thought of as a child's pastime, which of course it is. Yet, many adults have discovered creative expression in paperfolding, not only as an art, but with applications in education, engineering and even space exploration. Many schools include origami in the curriculum for math and science in elementary through high-school grades. Robert J. Lang (U.S.A.), a leading paperfolder, has devised software for creating origami models. Origami's universal appeal is firmly established.

PENGUIN
Florence Temko
U.S.A.

actual size

Paperfolders find origami to be a challenge and relaxation at the same time, whether they enjoy folding a simple toy or a complex animal form which could not have been imagined a few years ago. Innovative creators around the world have established reputations as visual artists by inventing entirely new techniques of manipulating pieces of paper.

In modular origami a number of similar units are folded in a set pattern and then combined into a compound structure. The sculptural parts, which give many contemporary origami models their representational qualities, are produced by folding with dampened paper — a process called wet-folding.

Technique, however is only a means. To be recognized as a work of art, an origami object must appeal to the viewer by conveying a sense of life. Origami forms speak to an observer because they demonstrate the creator's innate spirit reflected in the rich variations possible in a piece of paper.

PLEATED PATTERN
Florence Temko
U.S.A.

11 1/2" h

DISCOVERING PAPER

Michael G. La Fosse, Origamido Studio

When I first began to fold, the simple pleasure of transforming any kind of paper through origami was exhilarating. Wherever I went, I could find paper to entertain others, pass the time, or relax in the meditative aspects of just playing around with paper folding. The different textures, weights, colors and qualities of these common papers were interesting, and transforming any paper at hand into a bunny rabbit, a balloon or a paper airplane was magical to my friends. I loved the sound and the feel of working with the different types of common papers, and I was an eager experimenter — I learned a lot about paper in this way.

To a limited extent, I did try to match the paper to the subject. My limited palette included typing, tracing, wrapping, and grocery bag papers. I soon became more fussy about my choice of paper for each origami model. One kind of paper, crisp and lemon yellow, would become a canary; another sheet, chestnut and waxy smooth, became a crab. This was sufficient for a few years, or at least until the age of twelve.

Thanks to a *Reader's Digest* article about the artistry of origami master Akira Yoshizawa, I realized that my palette of papers was too limited, and that the type of paper was crucial to creating art from folded paper. As I stared at each of the photos in the article, I was amazed by the success of the expression that Yoshizawa folded into his models. What was the difference between his work and mine? It must be the paper. How and where did Yoshizawa come across such perfect papers?

I began my search for papers similar to the models in the magazine. My first stop was an art supply store, which carried a limited selection

WILBUR THE PIGLET
Michael G. La Fosse
U.S.A.

actual size

of thin, soft, white sheets of so-called rice papers, made in Asia. I purchased a few sheets and was promptly disappointed by the floppy result. There seemed to be nothing readily available between common papers and this mushy soft rice paper.

I recalled being on a field trip to a paper mill when I was an eight-year-old Cub Scout. The paper we made during the tour was crisp and strong, almost like a white version of a grocery bag. I could suddenly imagine myself making sharp creases and sculptural lines, similar to those in Yoshizawa's models. I needed to find out how that paper was made when we took that trip as Cub Scouts several years ago.

My home town, Fitchburg, Massachusetts, was a papermaking town. I soon befriended workers at the paper mill and devoured books about hand papermaking at the local libraries. By the age of sixteen, I was fully obsessed with making my own paper, with what now seems to be crude equipment.

Now I have my own design studio with a papermaking room. I can create any type of paper for my origami art, and often work with other origami artists to help them do the same.

VIEWPOINT ON ORIGAMI DESIGN

Robert J. Lang

Like most arts, origami achieves its unique character at least partly from the limitations of its medium. In the purest and most common form of the art, only a single square of paper is used. The image is formed by folding alone, no cutting allowed. This restriction gives origami a certain integrity; nothing is added, nothing is taken away. There is a continuous connection between the original, unfolded sheet and the finished form. In painting, the image is constructed by the discontinuous addition of color to the canvas; in carving, the image is achieved by selective removal. But in origami, you end up with what you started with. And yet, it is transformed in such a way that the plainest, most featureless of starting materials becomes complex, elegant, thought-provoking, or beautiful. This continuous transformation is an essential part of the allure of origami for many of its practitioners — including myself.

Such a tight restriction could have been the undoing of origami as an art — a relatively recent development within the multi-century-old tradition of paper folding. For most of its existence, origami, and paper-folding in general, was practiced primarily for functional or frivolous purpose, as wrapping, as decoration, as toy. Folding alone would not seem to allow for significant creative expression.

Within the last century, however, origami developed beyond its traditional roots. Its modern rebirth began when a Japanese metalworker named Akira Yoshizawa began creating new origami figures in the early 1930s and publicizing his work through books and exhibitions. He was joined by others in Japan, notably Isao Honda, Kosho and Michio Uchiyama, and Toyoaki Kawai. A worldwide

KABUTO MUSHI
Robert J. Lang
U.S.A.
3 1/4" l

expansion began in the 1950s with this new form of origami spreading to America, Great Britain, and beyond, connecting the rejuvenated Japanese art to preexisting local traditions of paperfolding. A burst of publication and popularization starting in the 1950s — notably by Harbin, Honda, Oppenheimer and Randlett, cemented the word origami (not universally used even in Japan) as the name of the activity and launched a wave of growth, expansion, and maturation of the art that continues unabated today. The fruits of this wave are the new designs of origami figures. In books, articles, convention programs and unpublished notes they number, conservatively, in the tens of thousands.

Those thousands of new designs would not have arisen if there had not been a parallel growth in the techniques of origami design. Fifty years ago all of the different origami designs in the world could have been catalogued on a single typed sheet of paper, had anyone had the inclination to do so. No model would have run over 20 or 30 steps. Most could be folded in a few minutes, even by a novice. Today, the most sophisticated designs have hundreds of steps and take several hours for an experienced folder to produce. The past 60 years in Japan, and 40 years worldwide, have seen a renaissance in the world of origami and an acceleration in its evolution.

How does a new origami design arise? Throughout the history of origami, most designers have created new figures by many approaches, ranging from simple trial-and-error to following a developed intuition about which steps to take to achieve a particular end. My own approach to design followed what I suspect is a not uncommon pattern; it evolved over the years from simply playing around with the paper, through somewhat more directed playing, to systematic folding.

I suspect that my own design evolution has paralleled the origami world at large, for now there are many codified techniques for design. By relating problems in origami design to simple geometrical concepts, it becomes

WESTERN POND TURTLE
Robert J. Lang
U.S.A.

actual size

possible to systematically produce origami structures. Using techniques with names like circle packing, square packing, rivers, tiling, and molecules, the origami designer can now produce flaps, body segments, layers, and textures: the building blocks of an origami subject.

Any budding origami designer almost inevitably develops some of the basic ideas underlying design simply through experimentation. Some are almost intuitively obvious. For example, "any given region of paper can only be used in one appendage." Another concept is "the paper cannot be stretched, only shortened, by folding." These two ideas can be used as rough guides to design, but they can also be expressed with mathematical rigor and clarity, even expressed as mathematical equations, and when so expressed, can be refined and sharpened into tools that can cut through the most complex and intractable design problem. Transforming one's thoughts from origami folding to geometrical concepts involves a certain level of abstraction, but it is a jump that many folders have taken and used to construct fantastically complex origami figures.

All origami designers bring elements of themselves to their designs. Over my life, my "origami" life and my "real" life as an engineer and physicist have intersected each other repeatedly, until they have become inextricably entangled. In recent years, this entanglement has led me to tap the language and investigative tools of physics to formulate origami design rules as formal mathematical equations. Shifting from geometrical concepts to mathematical equations is yet another step of abstraction, another step removed from the folding of paper. It is a curious thing that mathematical equations can be opaque, even forbiddingly intimidating, and yet can be used to clarify and sharpen a concept. I have found that once I have been able to express a design idea in equations, I could more readily use the underlying concept to achieve my own designs.

ALAMO STALLION
Robert J. Lang
U.S.A.
7" l

When designing a model by thought or pencil and paper, I usually use the concept, not the equation. One can discover a crease pattern for a collection of flaps by finding a packing of circles represented by the flaps; and, while such packings can be readily found by sketching, the equations that express the same problem are intractably difficult to solve — that is, by hand. A benefit of equations is that they can be solved by computer; and thus, in another overlap with my engineering background, I have developed a computer program based on the equations of origami design whose solutions generate origami crease patterns. It has been a project of several years, growing as I developed new and more powerful algorithms for origami design, and serving, in turn, as a testbed to refine and extend origami design ideas.

In its early years, the program could only find relatively simple bases which had already been discovered; but in recent years, my program, called *TreeMaker*, has become sufficiently powerful that it can find bases of far greater complexity and sophistication than I (or, I suspect, anyone) could devise working solely by hand. Using *TreeMaker*, I have created bases for a number of subjects whose solutions have eluded me over the years — deer with varying sizes and types of antlers, 32-legged, centipede-like creatures, flying insects, and more. Using a computer program accelerates the development of a model by orders of magnitude; from the tree to the full crease pattern can take less than five minutes, although folding the crease pattern into a base may take hours or days after that.

No one tool is all-purpose; I use intuition, geometrical concepts, equations, computer solutions and combinations thereof in my designs. Each is a tool, better for some tasks than others, and I choose the tool that seems best suited for the design problem at hand. As the use of geometrical design techniques has become more widespread in recent years, I have heard some people express reservations about using such tools in design — a fear, perhaps, that the tool could come to dominate the artist. This outcome seems unlikely to me. Rather, the tools of mathematical origami design allow an origami artist to more fully realize his or her vision, and to know in advance what the outcome of folding will be.

previous page

SWAN

4 5/8" h

SPARROW

above image actual size

Akira Yoshizawa

Japan

INTERNATIONALLY RECOGNIZED FATHER OF CONTEMPORARY ORIGAMI

opposite

HANNYA MASK
Akira Yoshizawa
Japan

actual size

pages 50-51

BANTAM COCK AND HEN
Akira Yoshizawa
Japan

actual size

GORILLA
Akira Yoshizawa
Japan

actual size

MASK OF BUDDHA
Seiji Nishikawa
Japan

actual size

WITCH
Seiji Nishikawa
Japan

actual size

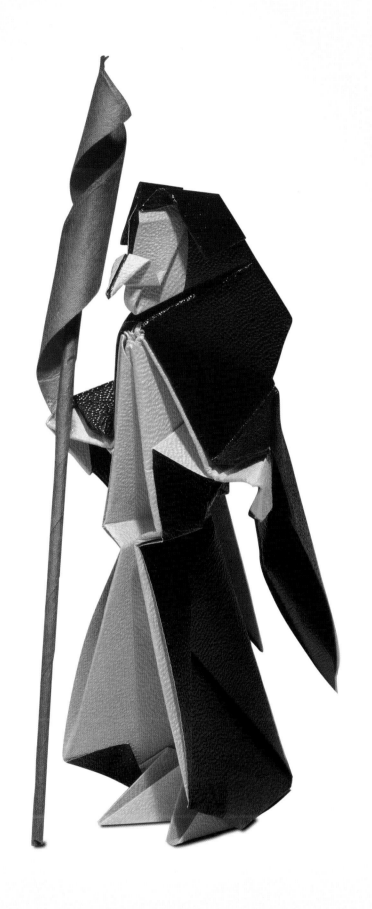

opposite

MUSK OX
Fumiaki Kawahata
Japan

actual size

pages 60 - 61

DIMETRON (DINOSAUR)
Fumiaki Kawahata
Japan

4 3/4" h

opposite

UNICORN

Fumiaki Kawahata

Japan

8 1/2" h

pages 64-65

PEGASUS

Fumiaki Kawahata

Japan

8 3/4" h

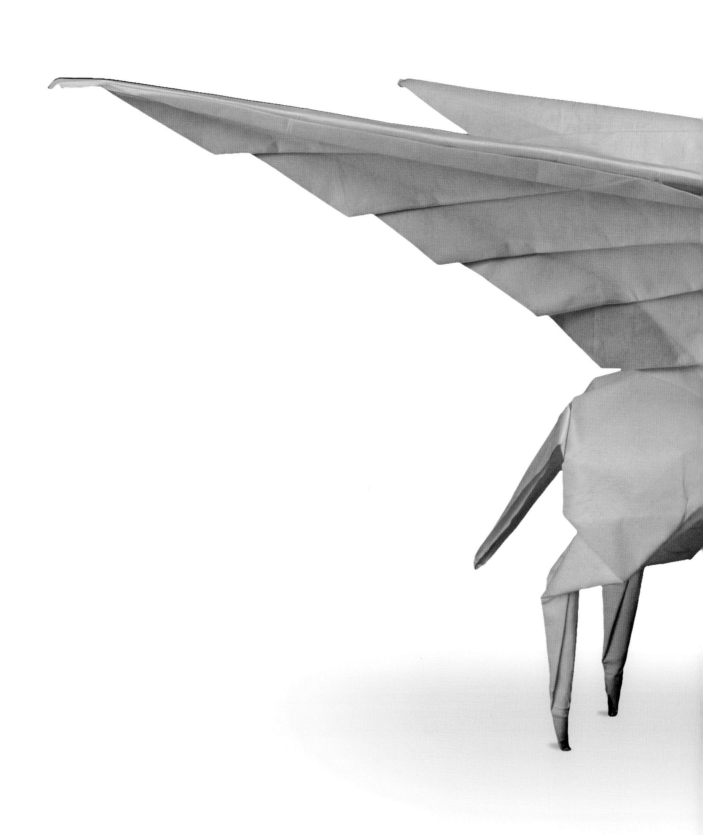

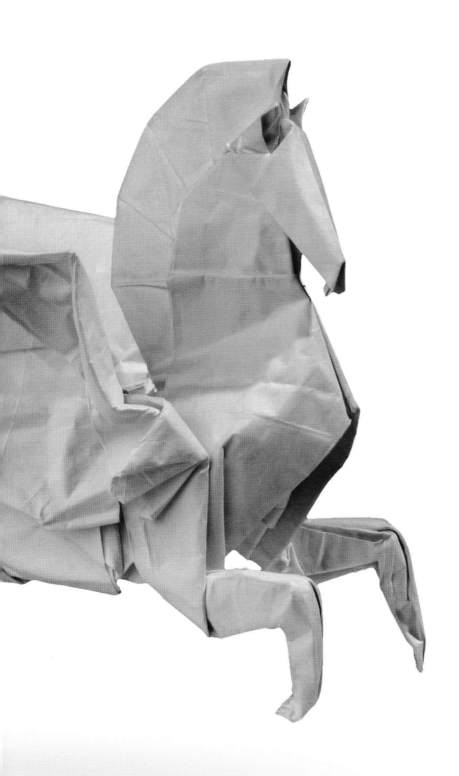

ANGEL PLAYING LUTE

Fumiaki Kawahata

Japan

actual size

WASP
Satoshi Kamiya
Japan

5 1/2" h

BAHAMUT
Satoshi Kamiya
Japan

actual size

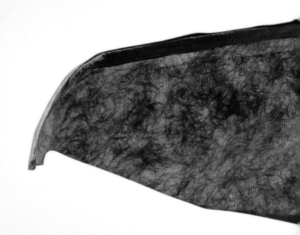

opposite

PTERANODON

Satoshi Kamiya

Japan

actual size

pages 78-79

DINOSAURS

Satoshi Kamiya

Japan

actual size

pages 80-81

WOOLY MAMMOTH

Satoshi Kamiya

Japan

actual size

pages 82-83

LION
Hideo Komatsu
Japan

actual size

opposite

COSMOSPHERE
Miyuki Kawamura
Japan

19 1/4" d

pages 86-87

COLLECTION OF LIDDED BOXES
Tomoko Fusé
Japan

actual size

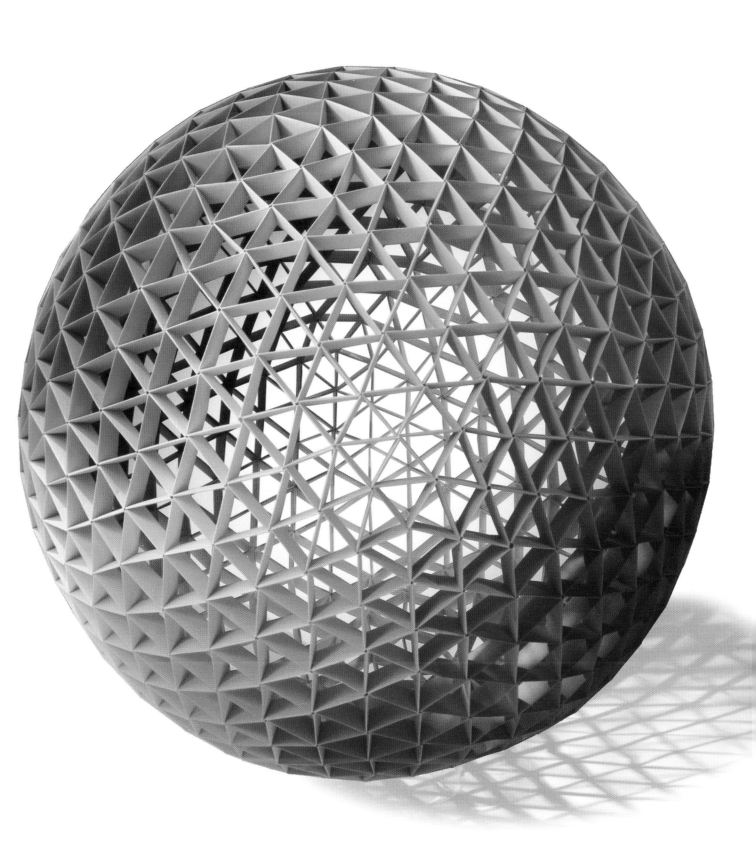

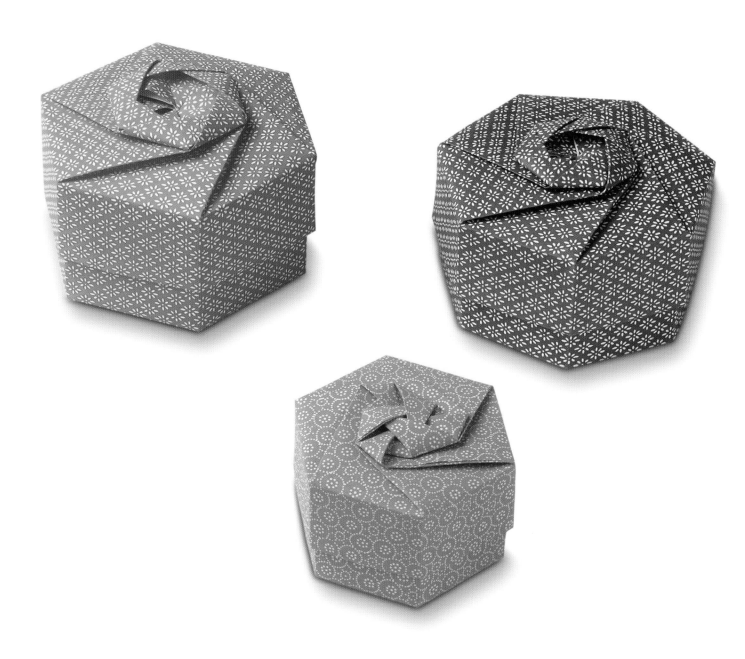

DEVIL

three papers used to create form

Joseph Wu

Canada

actual size

GOBLIN

two papers used to create form

Joseph Wu

Canada

actual size

UNICORN

two papers used to create form

Joseph Wu

Canada

actual size

HIPPOCAMPUS

three papers used to create form

Joseph Wu

Canada

9 1/4" h

ANGEL

three papers used to create form

Joseph Wu

Canada

actual size

BLACK BEAR
Joseph Wu
Canada

actual size

HORSE
Eric Joisel
France

7 1/8" h

SEAHORSE

Eric Joisel

France

13 7/8" h

MASK
Eric Joisel
France

11" h

MASK
Eric Joisel
France

15" h

MASK
Eric Joisel
France

9 1/2" h

ALONE ?
Fritz Junior Jacquet
France

actual size

photographs by Anthony Scoggins

page 116

TREE
Vincent Floderer
France

actual size

page 117

MORTERATSCH
Vincent Floderer
France

40 1/4 " h

opposite

SKULL
The lower jaws are a mirror reflection of the origami that forms the upper part of the skull.
Herman Van Goubergen
Belgium
folded by Koshiro Hatori

actual size

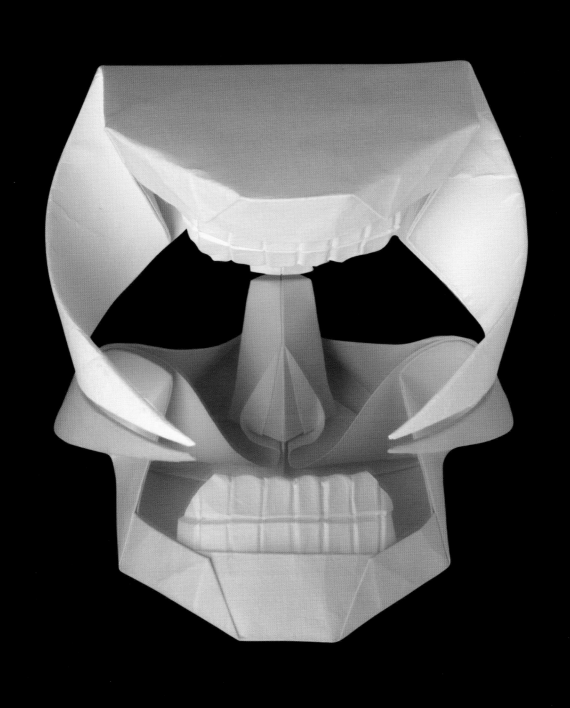

ELEGIE
Yuri and Katrin Shumakov
Russia

16 " h

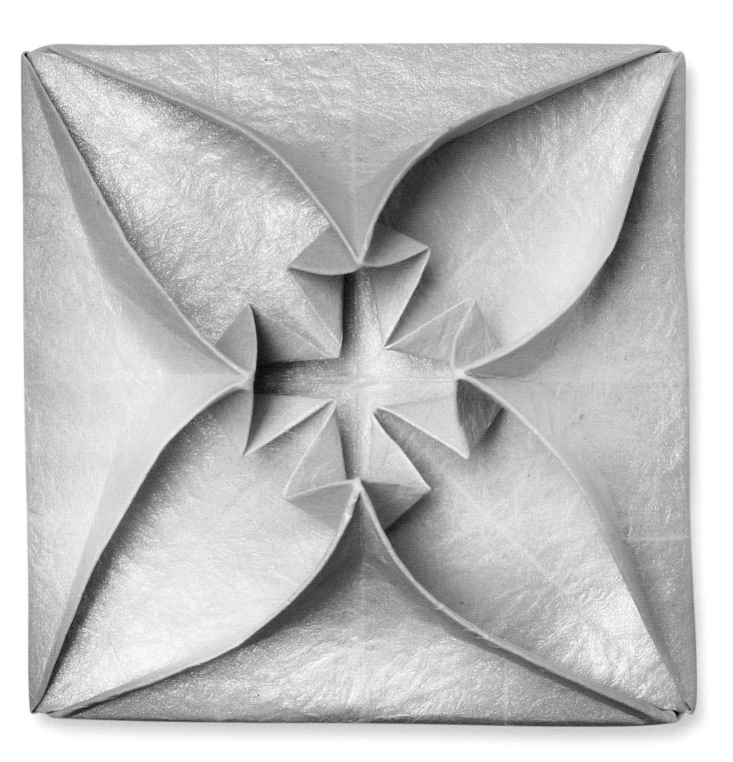

OWL

Nathan Geller

U.S.A.

actual size

photograph by Anthony Scoggins

OWL
Giang Dinh
U.S.A.

5 3/4" h

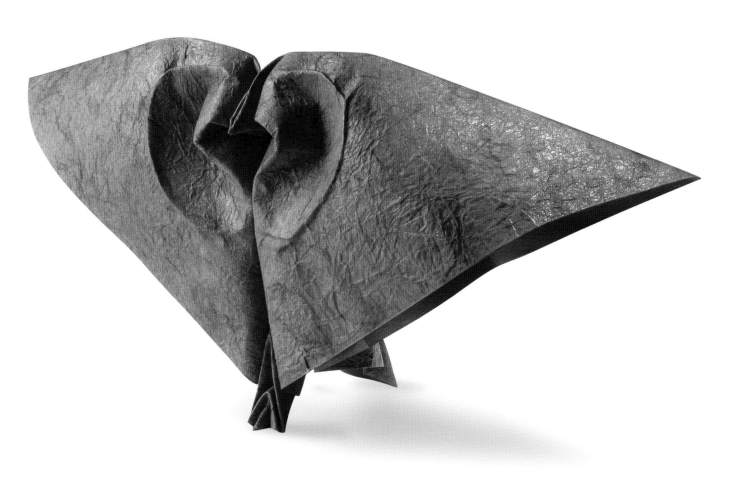

TAI CHI MASTER
Giang Dinh
U.S.A.

9 5/8" h

SEATED GUITARIST
Marc Kirschenbaum
U.S.A.

actual size

CERBERUS

Kentarou Fukuyama

Japan

actual size

photograph by Anthony Scoggins

page 140

ATLAS BEETLE

Daniel Robinson

U.S.A.

actual size

page 141

ELK

Daniel Robinson

U.S.A.

actual size

opposite

GEOMETRIC FORM - ORB

modular - 30 sheets

Jeannine Mosely

U.S.A.

6" d

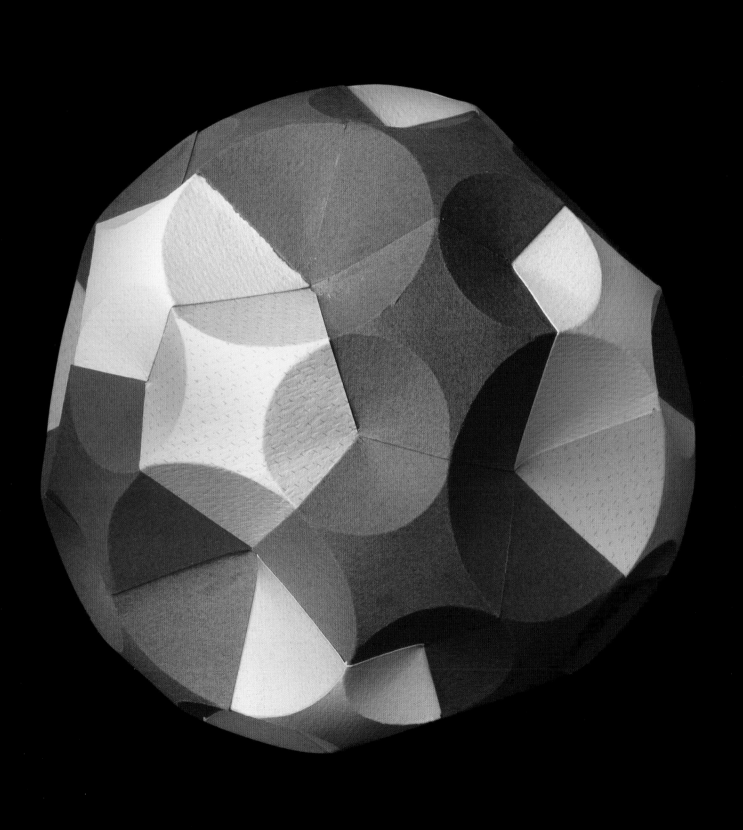

GEOMETRIC FORM - ARCTURUS

modular - 30 sheets

Jeannine Mosely

U.S.A.

actual size

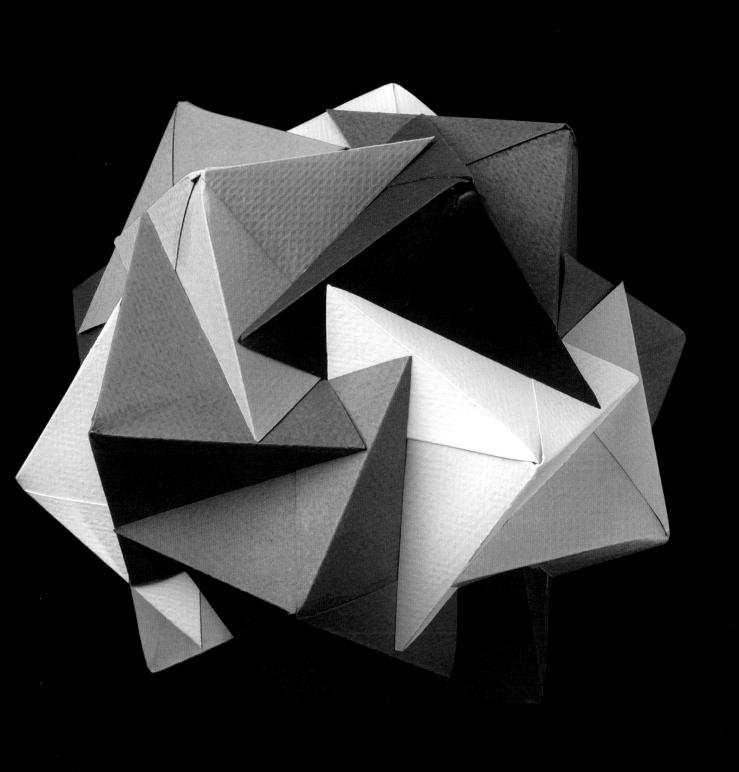

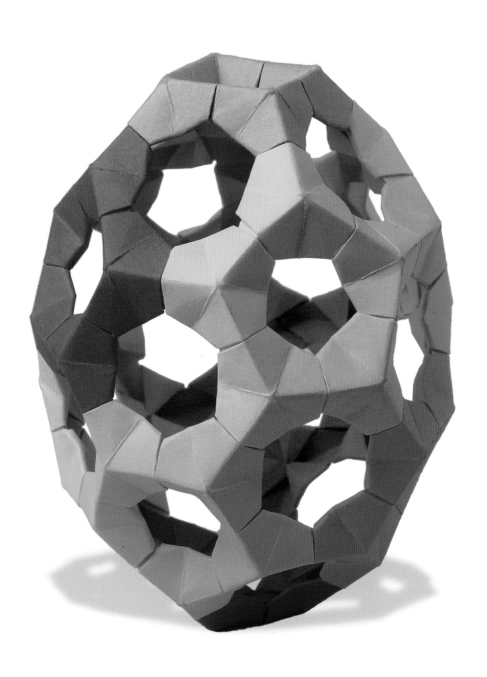

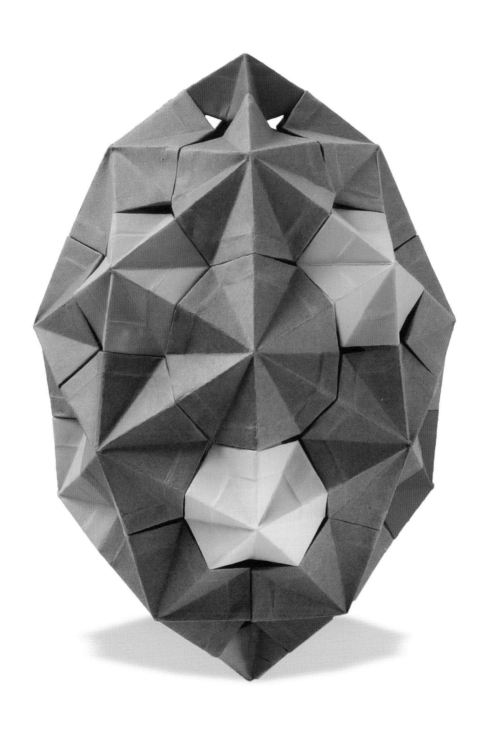

BIBLIOGRAPHY

Brill, David. *Brilliant Origami: A Collection of Original Design by David Brill*. Briarcliff Manor, NY: Japan Publications, 1995.

Fusé, Tomoko. *Origami Boxes*. Tokyo: Japan Publications Inc., Ltd., 1989.

Gurkewitz, Rona and Bennett Arnstein. *3-D Geometric Origami Modular Polyhedra*. Mineola: Dover Publications, Inc., 1995.

Hull, Thomas. (ed.). *Origami* [3]. Natick: A.K. Peters, Ltd., 2002.

Jackson, Paul. *Classic Origami*. New York: Mallard Press, 1990.

Kawahata, Fumiaki. *Origami Fantasy*. Tokyo: Origami House, 1995.

Kawasaki, Toshikazu. *Rose and Origami Mathematics*. Tokyo: Morikita Shuppan, 1998.

Kenneway, Eric. *Complete Origami*. New York: St. Martin's Press, 1987.

Kirschenbaum, Mark (ed.). *2003 Origami Collection*. New York: OrigamiUSA, 2003.

Kunihiko Kasahara and Toshie Takahama, (eds.). *Origami for the Connoisseur*. Tokyo: Japan Publications, Inc., 1987.

Lang, Robert, J. *Origami Design Secrets: Mathematical Methods for an Ancient Art*. Natick: A.K. Peters, Ltd., 2003.

opposite

BULL

Kim Sang-Heun

Korea

actual size

photograph by Anthony Scoggins

pages 152-153

KNIGHT ON DRAGON

Noboru Miyajima

Japan

6" h

page 154

HORSE

David Brill

England

6 7/8" h

—. *Origami in Action: Paper Toys that Fly, Flap, Gobble, and Inflate*. New York: St. Martin's Griffin, 1997.

—. *Origami Insects and Their Kin: Step-by-Step Instructions in over 1500 Diagrams*. New York: Dover Publications, 1995.

—. *Origami Insects II* (Origami Zukan Konchu 2). Tokyo: Origami House, 2003.

Montroll, John. *Easy Origami*. New York: Dover Publications, 1992.

—. *Teach Yourself Origami*. Maryland: Antroll Publications, 1998.

—. *Bringing Origami to Life*. New York: Dover Publications, 1999.

Nishikawa, Seiji. *Works of Seiji Nishikawa*. Tokyo: Origami House, 2003.

Temko, Florence. *Origami For Beginners*. Boston: Tuttle Publishing, 2002.

—. *Origami Boxes and More*. Boston: Tuttle Publishing, 2003.

—. *Origami Toys*. Boston: Tuttle Publishing, 2003.

—. *Paper Pandas and Jumping Frogs*. San Francisco: China Books & Periodicals, 1986.

Yamaguchi, Makoto. *Practical Origami*. Tokyo: Natsume Sha, 2003.

—. *LET'S ENJOY ORIGAMI*. Tokyo: Ikeda Shoten Publishing Co., 2001.

Yamaguchi, Makoto (ed.). *Origami Insects* (Origami Zukan Konchu 1). Tokyo: Origami House, 2000.

Yoshizawa, Akira. *Compilation Of Masterworks By Yoshizawa Akira (Nochi Yutaka Na Origami)*. Tokyo: Sojusha, 1996.

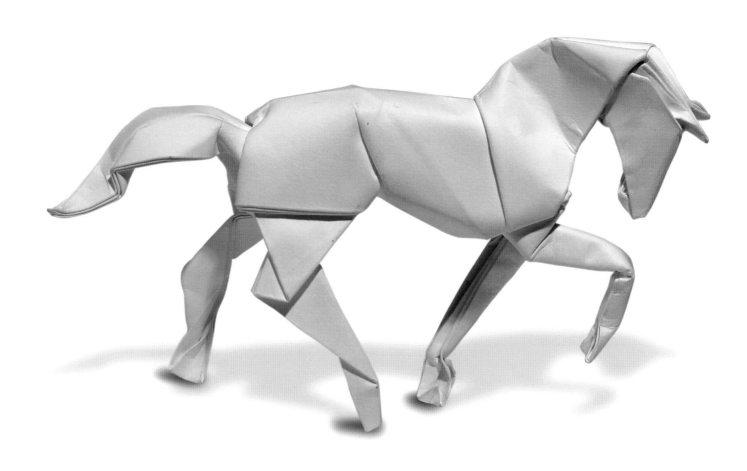

DIRECTOR'S CIRCLE
Members who provide core support for the Museum's exhibitions

Ron & Mary Taylor, Chairmen

Mr. & Mrs. Oscar Ancira

Mr. & Mrs. Augusto Angelucci

Mrs. Frances M. Armstrong

Barbara Baehr

Mr. & Mrs. Bob Baker

Mrs. Ina Bartell

Carolyn L. E. Benesh & Robert K. Liu

Dr. & Mrs. H. Kenneth Bishop

Mr. Norman Blachford

Dr. James Lewis Bowers

Ms. Clara Jo Brown

Ms. Esther J. Burnham

Louisa Campagna

Mr. & Mrs. Hugh C. Carter

Drs. William & Marsha Chandler

Mr. & Mrs. Jack Charney

Mrs. Jacques Clerk

Mrs. James W. Colachis

Mr. & Mrs. Richard K. Colbourne

Dr. Roger C. Cornell

Mr. & Mrs. Donald F. Craib, Jr.

Mr. & Mrs. Christopher Cramer

Mr. & Mrs. Lawrence M. Cushman

Nancy N. Danninger

Mr. & Mrs. Alex De Bakcsy

Dr. & Mrs. Anthony DeMaria

Mr. & Mrs. Michael H. Dessent

Mr. & Mrs. A. C. Duckett

Jack & Lorrain Duffy

Mr. & Mrs. Karl Eller

Mr. Peter C. Farrell & Ms. Fiona Tudor

Kathryn Fishback & Jeanne Jones

Ms. Joan Fisher

Annette & Dick Ford

Judith S. Fox & Edmund F. Ackell

Debbie & Mitchell Friedlaender

Mr. & Mrs. Orrin Gabsch

Mr. & Mrs. George Gafford

Mr. & Mrs. William Geiger

Mr. & Mrs. Arnold Ginnow

Joyce & Edward Glazer

Mrs. Milton D. Goldberg

Mrs. Connie K. Golden

Mrs. Betty Gouraud

Mr. & Mrs. Walter Green

Nathelle M. Greenleaf

Mr. & Mrs. Ernest Hahn, II

Mr. & Mrs. Ronald E. Hahn

Mr. & Mrs. William M. Hawkins, Jr.

Mr. & Mrs. Richard C. Helmstetter

Mr. & Mrs. Lionel P. Hernholm, Jr.

Mr. William E. Heyler

Ken & Sandy High

Mrs. Kenneth E. Hill

Dr. Maryalys K. Hill

Dr. & Mrs. Stuart Jamieson

Kristin E. Jeffery

Mr. Gary Jugum

Mr. Maurice M. Kawashima

Allison Kelly / Qualcomm

Mr. & Mrs. Ronald H. Kendrick

Mr. & Mrs. Neil A. Kjos, Jr.

Mr. & Mrs. Frederick Kleinbub

Mr. & Mrs. Gene R. Konrad

Phyllis & Martin Kornfeld

Dr. & Mrs. Jay Kovtun

Mr. & Mrs. George Lazarnick

Mr. & Mrs. Marvin Levine

Mr. & Mrs. William Mackenzie

Lani & Herb McCoy

Mr. & Mrs. James F. Mulvaney

Mr. & Mrs. Walter Munk

Tracy & Andy Nelson

Mr. & Mrs. William Norgren

Mr. George M. Pardee, Jr.

Tom & Karen Pecht

Mrs. George Peterson

Mrs. Walter J. Podbielniak

Mr. & Mrs. Hughes Potiker

Diane Powers

Dr. Jeffrey Pressman & Dr. Nancy Kollisch

Mr. & Mrs. Sol Price

Mr. & Mrs. Elliott Rabin

Phil & Pam Reed

Mr. Edward H. Richard &

   Mr. Warren P. Kendrick

Gene & Lydia Roberts

Mr. Jeremiah Robins

Charlie Robins

Ewa Robinson

RADM & Mrs. W. Haley Rogers

Mrs. William C. Ruzich

Dr. & Mrs. Joseph D. Schmidt

Victor Sell

Letitia J. Sherman

Donald & Darlene Shiley

Guy Showley & Jo Bobbie MacConnell

Mr. John R. Siglow

Dr. Robert Singer & Ms. Judith Harris

Jim & Norma Slone

Mr. & Mrs. Joel Sollender

Mrs. Worley Stewart

Mrs. Gwen Stoughton

Mary Ann & Bob Stubbs

Ms. Deborah Szekely

Mr. & Mrs. J. L. Tanzer

Ms. Florence Temko

Mr. & Mrs. Terry Thomas

The John M. & Sally B.

   Thornton Foundation

Nancy B. Tieken

Dr. & Mrs. Andrew Viterbi

Barbara Walbridge

Mary G. Walker

Dr. & Mrs. Robert D. Wallace

Dr. & Mrs. Tom A. Waltz

Mr. & Mrs. John H. Warner, Jr.

Mr. Lewis Warner

Mr. & Mrs. Howard Weiner

Mr. & Mrs. Louis Weinstock

Mr. & Mrs. Jean-René Westfall

The Frederic & Eileen Monaghan

   Whitaker Foundation

Ms. Therese T. Whitcomb

Mr. & Mrs. Harold B. Williams

Mr. & Mrs. Robert K. Wolford

Richard & Kaye Woltman

Elizabeth & Joe Yamada

Ms. Carolyn Yorston

Mr. & Mrs. Walter J. Zable

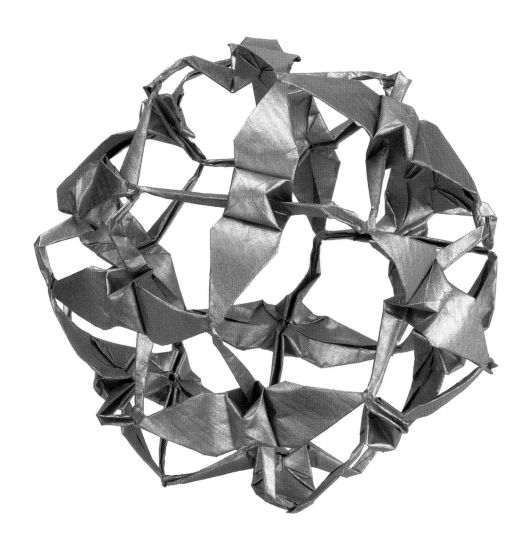

Mingei International Museum is a non-profit, public foundation.
It is dedicated to furthering understanding of historical and
contemporary art of the people from all cultures of the world —
so that they may be inspired to express their own innate creativity.

The Museum is supported by memberships and contributions. The museum
program is funded in part by the City of San Diego Commission for Arts
and Culture and the County of San Diego Community Enhancement Program.

Telephone: (619) 239-0003   Fax: (619) 239-0605   Website: www.mingei.org

PUBLICATION

Design and Editing	MARTHA W. LONGENECKER
Editing	ROB SIDNER
Photography	LYNTON GARDINER
Media Production	ANTHONY SCOGGINS
Production Coordinator	V'ANN CORNELIUS
Production Assistants	TERRI BRYSON
	CATHERINE HERBIN
	GRETCHEN VAN CAMP
	VICKY MIHARA AVERY
Typesetting	WESTERFIELD TYPESETTING & GRAPHICS
Printing	PARTNER PRESS

opposite

PEACE SPHERE

incorporating Rokoan style - one paper

Linda Mihara

U.S.A.

actual size

page 160

FIVE INTERSECTING TETRAHEDRA

modular - 30 sheets

Thomas Hull

U.S.A.

actual size